GREECE

Children of Other Lands

Jill Golick

 Grolier

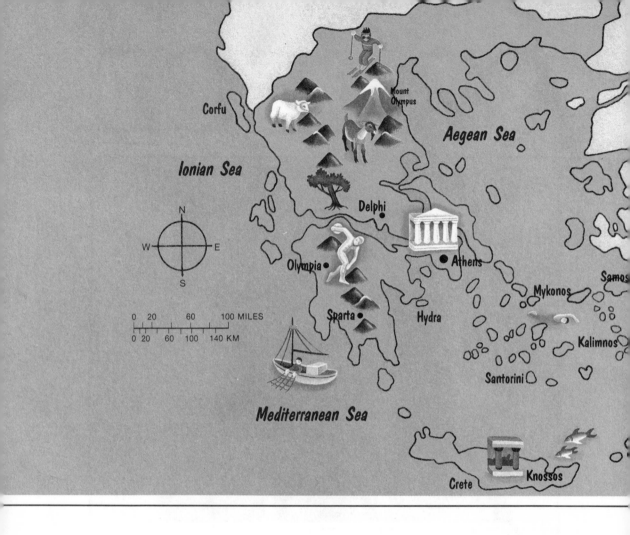

This library reinforced edition is available exclusively from:

Grolier Educational Corporation
Sherman Turnpike, Danbury, Connecticut 06816

Contents

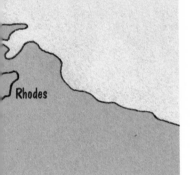

Rhodes

Have you ever wondered how the Olympic Games got their name? They are named for Olympia, a place in Greece where the first Olympic Games were held almost 3000 years ago. Those very first "games" actually consisted of only one race—a short sprint— and the prize was a wreath of olive leaves. Over the years the number of events increased to include everything from chariot races to trumpet competitions.

The Olympic Games have spread far and wide from Greece. They are now held once every four years in different locations all over the world. The official sports range from cycling to judo and ice-dancing to bob-sledding, sports the ancient Greeks never even dreamed of. But the modern world still acknowledges its debt to Greece for the ideals of peace, athletic excellence and sportsmanship that inspired the Games. The Greek team always leads the opening parade and the Olympic flame is still lit at Olympia and brought all the way from there to the site of the Games.

What kind of a country provided the world with the Olympic Games? Greece is a land of ancient traditions, classical architecture, colorful myths and, some say, the most beautiful beaches and friendliest people in the world. Let's find out what it's like to grow up in such a place.

Tomorrow's champions?

Mountain Islands

Round the world, there are folk tales about the way the world began and how particular countries came to be. One that Greek kids sometimes hear tells how God, after making the oceans and continents, took a big bag of rocks and sprinkled them around to make hills and mountains. But the bag broke over Greece, showering the land with mountains and creating hundreds of islands in the surrounding seas.

Believe that tale or not, there's no denying that from almost anywhere you stand in Greece you can see a mountain. And if you climb to the top of it, you might be able to see some of the 1400 islands that dot the waters around the mainland. Many of those islands are the peaks of mountain ranges, and some, like Santorini, still have active volcanoes.

Although three seas—the Mediterranean, the Ionian and the Aegean—lap at the Greek coastline, most of the land is dry and rocky. Much of the country has very hot summers when little or no rain falls. The rest of the year in these areas is mild, and there is some rain from October to March. Central and northern areas, however, have colder winters. The mountains there become covered in snow—perfect for skiing.

The village of Thira, on the island of Santorini.

When's Your Name Day?

These girls might be named Katerina and Maria or Eleni and Alexandra, all very popular names for girls.

In case you were wondering . . . Some favorite names for boys are Giorgios, Michalis, Kostas and Yannis.

Are you named after anyone? If you lived in Greece, you most likely would be. In Greek families, the eldest daughter is often named after her father's mother and the eldest son after his father's father. The second born daughter and son are named after their mother's parents.

Whether or not Greek kids share their name with a relative, they often share it with an Orthodox saint, a historical figure, a god or goddess. Boys may be Sokratis after the famous philosopher or Alexandros after Alexander the Great. Girls may be called Athina or Demetra after the goddesses.

But most kids think having a saint's name is best because then they get to celebrate not just one but *two* special days of their own—their birthday and their "name day." July 25, for instance, is St. Anne's day and a special day for every Anna in Greece. Boys called Dimitri are excited on October 26, the day of St. Dimitrios. Friends drop by on name days to visit and enjoy food, music and dancing together, and to wish Anna or Dimitri "many years."

Make Yourself at Home

In the cities and big towns of Greece most families live in apartment buildings. In general, apartments are not very large. They usually have only a living room with attached kitchen, a bathroom and one or two bedrooms.

White-washed houses with flat roofs are common throughout the small towns and villages. Most of these are small as well. Many do not have backyards like North American houses. Instead, in areas where there is enough rain, homes may have a courtyard open to the sky filled with plants and flowers—the perfect place to play. On some of the Aegean islands houses are built very close together, sometimes almost one on top of another, as protection from storms. Kids play in the narrow passageways and streets in these towns.

Some Greek kids are lucky enough to have their very own bedroom, but most share a room with a brother or sister. Sometimes grandparents or an unmarried uncle or aunt live with the family. This is not as common as it used to be, however, especially in the cities. There, usually only mom, dad and kids live together.

Dazzling white-washed walls are characteristic of houses in many parts of Greece.

Did you know . . .
White is by far the favorite color for houses on the Greek islands, but shutters, window frames and doors are often painted bright colors, with blue probably the most popular.

The Parthenon is one of the most famous buildings in the world. Built on a hill called the Acropolis, it was a temple dedicated to Athena, the goddess of wisdom and the patron of Athens.

City Sights

Kids in Athens may live in an ultra modern apartment building and play tag nearby between columns 2500 years old. The capital is the largest city in Greece and is home to almost one-third of the population of the entire country. It is also one of the oldest cities in the world. Looking down from the top of one of the many hills dotting Athens you can see both ancient ruins and brand new office towers.

There are many exciting places for kids to explore. The twisting streets below the Parthenon are perfect for hide-and-seek. Or you can go to the Parliament Building to watch the presidential guards in kilts with great pom-poms on their shoes. A visit to one of the many parks provides a break from all the hustle and bustle of the crowded city, and after that you can check out the wares of the many street vendors who sell tasty snacks and all kinds of toys.

A quick trip to the port of Piraeus at the edge of Athens provides lots of action. There are always huge freighters loading and unloading, and gleaming white ferries and cruise ships docking. If it gets too hot and noisy you can always hop on the subway, or metro as Greeks call it, to head home. And when evening falls maybe mom and dad will take you to an open air movie theater under the stars as a special treat.

Village Ways

Most North Americans have an idea of Greece that comes from books they've read and movies they've seen. They know that Athens is a big, modern city, but think of the rest of the country as a series of picturesque farming and fishing villages, where people dress and live in old-fashioned ways and where donkeys are the main means of transportation.

Actually, Greece has changed a lot in the last 10 or 20 years, and life in most Greek villages is now very similar to city life. It is somewhat quieter and slower paced, but you'll see more T-shirts and track suits than long skirts and kerchiefs, and more cars and motor scooters than donkeys. And chances are that any donkeys you do see are there mainly because tourists expect them!

There are some remote villages, however, where life has not changed all that much—and even a few where people do get around on donkeys. Everyone knows everyone else, and there are usually a few tables and chairs in the village square where people gather in the evenings to play backgammon and talk. Most families have a bit of land to farm, maybe a few olive or almond trees, and a few animals. Kids get up early to feed the chickens and goat, and at harvest time all family members and even neighbors come to help.

Friendly Family

When dad comes home from a long day's work, kids spend as much time with him as they can.

In case you were wondering . . .
The average Greek family today has two kids.

It is said that if you insult one member of a Greek family, you have insulted them all. Families stick together and look after each other. And that doesn't just mean mom, dad, brothers and sisters. Cousins, aunts, uncles and grandparents are all loyal to the other members of their family.

Proper behavior is very important to Greeks, so it won't surprise you to learn that parents may be strict. However, kids are taken seriously and regularly join in adult conversation and activities. They are not told to go off and play and leave the grownups in peace.

Often both parents work, and kids are therefore expected to help out whenever possible. This may mean keeping the house tidy, helping prepare meals, serving customers at the family store or tending animals on the family farm. Many people have jobs in hotels, restaurants, souvenir and craft shops and other businesses related to tourism. Some work in the shipping industry, others in factories and offices, and others as farmers and fishermen. However, mom is much more likely to be a teacher or civil servant than dad.

The Freshest Ever

Easter bread fresh from the oven . . . could you resist?

In Greece, when city kids go grocery shopping with their parents, they often head for the nearest supermarket just as you might. But even in cities, many Greeks prefer to go to small shops and the market to buy fresh food. If they time their visit to the bakery right, the bread may still be warm, and the owner of the butcher shop will cut their meat exactly the way they like it. Some people even go out of their way to shop at a store they've always gone to, where they know they'll get the best possible price and the freshest food.

Open-air markets are especially fun to visit. Brightly colored goods are spread on tables and you can often bargain for a lower price. Athens has a famous flea market held every Sunday where you can buy handicrafts from all over the country: embroidered blouses, wool sweaters, pottery and jewelry as well as lots of second-hand goods.

If you cannot find what you are looking for anywhere else, try the local kiosk. There are thousands of these tiny street corner shops throughout the country, each one crammed with an incredible selection of items ranging from erasers and shoelaces to tape measures, magazines, string and just about everything else.

A Taste of Greece

After all that shopping, you will probably be hungry.
There are plenty of places to stop for a snack and there
are lots of delicious foods just right for eating while
you walk. Street vendors sell small flaky pies filled
with spinach and cheese, and skewers of barbecued
meat, called *souvlaki*. Or you could get a paper bag
full of hot fried potatoes or a grilled cob of corn. A
handful of pistachio nuts might be nice.

Greeks eat lots of lamb, seafood and vegetables. But
they eat one food more than any other: olive oil. Olive
oil is used for frying and for salads—Greeks hardly
cook a thing without it!

Greece is famous for many dishes. *Moussaka* is a
custardy casserole with eggplant, tomatoes, cheese and
ground meat. To make *dolmades*, you roll rice and
meat up in the leaves from grape vines and you eat
them leaves and all! *Feta* is a popular cheese often
made from sheep's milk. The most famous dish with
feta in it is the village salad, known by foreigners as
Greek salad: tomatoes, onions, olives and feta topped
with herbs and what else? You guessed it—olive oil. If
you are still hungry, try some *baklava*, a delicious
pastry stuffed with nuts and drenched in honey. Be
warned, you will have awfully sticky fingers when you
are done.

*What do you do when
you run out of hands?
You use your head, of
course.*

Did you know . . .
If a family has olive
trees, Greek kids know
better than to pop a
freshly picked one into
their mouth. Straight
from the tree, olives are
small, hard and very
bitter.

Eating Out

Especially during tourist season, many narrow streets are so filled with tables and diners that there's hardly room left to get by.

Would you believe ... About 8.5 million tourists visit Greece every year.

How often do you get to go to a restaurant with your family? If you lived in Greece, you would probably eat out once a week.

Greek restaurants are relaxed, friendly places. Waiters and waitresses know their regular customers by name, and best of all, you are almost always invited to the kitchen to take a peek into each pot. The cook will explain exactly what everything is and then you can order whatever looks good. Maybe you'd like to try the octopus stew or squid rings. Or would you prefer roast lamb or pork? No matter what you choose, it will be fresh and delicious.

As well as restaurants, cafés are popular places to go. In small communities, it's usually only men who gather there for small cups of strong coffee and conversation. However, entire families in cities and towns often go to cafés, especially those with outdoor tables, to have a drink, watch passersby and chat.

Off to School

Generally speaking, school in Greece starts at 8:00 or 8:30 with a prayer, often in the schoolyard. Then it's indoors to begin classes. There's a lot to learn, including the Greek language, math, science, geography and Greece's long, long history. Kids are happy when it's time for something fun like mythology, traditional crafts, art, folk dancing, recess or gym.

Classes are over for the day around 2 P.M. At least, they are if you are in the morning shift. In some cities the schools are too small to fit all the neighborhood children. So some kids go to school in the morning and others in the late afternoon.

Greek kids begin at age six at a *demotiko*, or elementary school. After six years they go on to a *gymnasio*, a three-year junior high school which is nothing like your gymnasium. Many students spend three more years at the *lycio*, studying hard for the entrance examinations to university. Others go to technical or vocational schools to learn to do different jobs. University is only for the best students and the exams are very, very difficult. Once you get in though, tuition and books are free, and needy students get an allowance for food and maybe even a free place to live!

It's All Greek to Me

Did you know that Greek is one of the oldest languages spoken in Europe? Well it is, and many of the other languages of Europe have borrowed a lot of Greek words. Among English words that come from Greek are comedy, octopus, zoo, democracy, grammar and telephone, to mention just a few. The list could go on and on.

Open a Greek book and you will not recognize many of the letters. There are 24 of them in the Greek alphabet rather than the 26 you are used to. Most of them look quite different from the letters in this book, which uses the Latin alphabet, and you can't even trust some of those that look the same. For instance, the Greek letter *P* represents the sound we write as *R*. And while you are safe with capital *M* and *N*, the lower case forms look confusingly like our *u* and *v*.

Because tourism is so important in Greece, a lot of street and shop signs are printed in both the Greek and Latin alphabets. Partly for the same reason, Greek kids may start studying English in school from as early as grade 3 or 4.

Now that you know a little bit about Greek, can you tell what this girl is writing? If you said "Anna," you're absolutely right.

Once Upon a Time

The first thing Greek kids study in history is mythology. And what a great way to learn about the past! These ancient legends of gods, goddesses and heroes are exciting, action-packed and colorful.

Greek myths center on a family of superhuman beings who lived on Mount Olympus long ago. You may have heard of Zeus, the king of the gods, who ruled with a thunder bolt. Poseidon, the brother of Zeus, could make storms at sea when he was grumpy. Eros flew through the air shooting magical arrows at people to make them fall in love. While some gods helped humans—Athena, for instance, the goddess of wisdom—others, like Ares, were always making trouble. There were all sorts of amazing creatures too, such as Pegasus, the flying horse, and centaurs, who were half-man and half-horse.

As well as gods and fabulous creatures, there were many Greek heroes with amazing skills. Achilles had been dipped in a magic river so he could not be harmed. Unfortunately his heel wasn't protected and an arrow hit his one weak spot. Heracles performed 12 seemingly impossible labors, including killing a lion with his bare hands.

Ancient urns were often decorated with scenes from mythology.

It's a Tough Life— or Is It?

Do you sometimes think you have it pretty rough— parents too strict, too much to study, too many chores to do? Well, Greek kids sometimes think that way too —at least until they learn in history class what life was like for the boys of Sparta back 2500 or so years ago.

In those days, each Greek city was like a separate country. The most important were Athens and Sparta, and they had very different ideas about almost everything. War was all-important to Spartans and boys started training for it when they were only seven years old. And what training! They left their families and went to live in barracks where they spent most of their time learning to wrestle, run and handle weapons. They had to do exercises outside no matter what the weather—and without any clothes on! They were often made to sleep outside too and were fed only the plainest food—and as little as would keep them healthy.

The boys in ancient Athens got a very different education. They learned to read, to play the lute, do math and recite poetry. With such different attitudes, it's not surprising that war broke out between Athens and Sparta—or that Sparta won. Or that, meanwhile, Athens was producing some of the most beautiful monuments and works of art and some of the greatest thinkers and writers the world has ever known.

Afternoon Adventures

After school, most Greek kids dash home for lunch. If their parents are working and can't get home, the kids may eat with a relative or a babysitter. Then they probably help with the dishes and take care of any chores they are responsible for.

Now comes the big decision: fun first or get the homework out of the way? On some days, though, there may not be any choice as many Greek kids take extra lessons after regular school. Some study English or French, others take art or ballet or learn to play a musical instrument—perhaps the bouzouki, a Greek instrument something like a mandolin.

But it's a long afternoon—dinner isn't until around 8:00—so whatever else kids have to do there's always some time for fun.

Greek kids enjoy many of the same things you do. Indoors, they watch TV—cartoons and sports are their favorites—play video games and board games and sometimes (probably not as often as their parents would like) just curl up with a good book. Outside, they go bike riding and skateboarding, they skip and fly kites and play hopscotch and ball with their friends.

Many live near a beach and spend a lot of time there, while others may go for long rambling walks in the hills. Still others may spend an afternoon or so a week

Practice makes perfect.

practicing the folk dances they learn in gym class at school. Some kids participate in festivals where they dress in traditional costumes and can show off their fancy footwork. But it takes lots of time and practice to get the steps just right.

Good Sports

Put a few kids, a ball and a bit of space together, and you've got a soccer game.

Baseball diamonds and hockey rinks are few and far between in Greece, but soccer is everywhere! *Podosphero*, or soccer, is everyone's favorite. In fields and village squares, you can almost always see kids kicking around soccer balls. If there is no one to play with, they practice bouncing the ball from knee to knee and from knee to head. Soccer leagues begin with kids aged six and continue up to university. When there aren't any live games to see the whole family crowds around the TV to watch professional soccer matches.

If a school has a playground, it probably has a basketball hoop in it. And if there is a hoop, there are kids shooting baskets. There are pick-up games at the end of the day and the entire school comes out to cheer when a school team has a game. Basketball is second only to soccer in Greece, and volleyball is also a favorite, especially with girls.

As well as team sports most kids love swimming. They often learn how from an older brother, sister or cousin. And if there is a boat around, the same relative might teach them to water-ski or sail.

Celebrate!

The Greek calendar is full of special days devoted to singing, dancing and feasting. There are cherry, theater and flower festivals, and carnivals complete with chariot parades. There are also many religious celebrations.

Christmas is a holiday especially for kids. On December 24 and 31 and January 6 they go from house to house singing carols in exchange for money and candy. There are no gifts on Christmas. But don't worry, there are presents on New Year's Day, which Greeks call St. Basil's Day.

Just before Lent, which lasts for seven weeks prior to Easter, is another time for celebrating. Kids dress up in colorful costumes to join the parades, carnivals, masquerade parties and feasts. The first day of Lent is Shrove Monday when Greek skies fill with kites. Families go on picnics into the country and kids compete to see whose kite will fly the highest. Lent is a time of prayer and often fasting. Then, in the evening on Holy Saturday the whole family attends an outdoor mass. At midnight everyone lights a candle before going home for a special lamb soup. On Easter Sunday the delicious smell of roasting lamb is everywhere as families gather for a feast and kids crack open the red-painted hard-boiled Easter eggs to let out the blessings.

Easter procession on the island of Patmos.

Did you know . . .
On St. Basil's Day most families serve a special cake with a coin in it. Whoever gets the piece with the coin will have good luck all year.

Hooray for the Holidays

Greeks have an old saying for most occasions and they have one for vacations too: "Greece is so beautiful, you never have to leave." Summer holidays are often spent visiting relatives in the village where mom and dad grew up. You might travel by plane, car, train or bus, but there are still some places you can only reach by boat or donkey!

Beaches and mountains are also popular for holidays. However, do not expect to find a quiet place all to yourself. During the summer vacation cities and towns empty as families head to the countryside and the islands. Favorite spots can get very crowded, especially when there are also foreign travelers visiting.

But most Greeks do not seem to get too upset by cramped conditions. This may be due to their love of talking. Grownups gather to discuss the problems of the world, their kids and, of course, politics. Kids like to talk about sports, the latest hit songs, their parents and, surprisingly, politics. And what better time for discussions than during a vacation when you can talk all night if you want to.

The more the merrier!

In case you were wondering . . . Summer holidays for Greek kids last from mid-June to mid-September.

Jewels of the Sea

The island of Patmos is important in Christian history. According to tradition, St. John the Evangelist spent two years in a grotto on Patmos, and it was there that he dictated The Book of Revelation, part of the New Testament, to a disciple. The monastery founded and named in his honor in 1088 can be seen in the distance.

Of the 1400 islands scattered in the waters around the Greek mainland, only 160 are inhabited. Because they are surrounded by water, each has developed its own special character and identity.

The island of Mykonos is one of the most famous. It has shining white houses, narrow streets and a church for each day of the year—365 in all! Kalimnos is known for its brave sponge divers who leave each year in the spring to collect sponges from the bottom of the sea off the coast of North Africa. One of the most northerly islands, Corfu, is a popular haven for tourists. Its red-domed Church of St. Spyridon is said to have special powers. Hydra is unusual because no cars are allowed to disturb the quiet of the peaceful island filled with red-roofed houses. Samos is one of the few islands with thick woods, and its ancient port, which is no longer in use, is named after a famous mathematician, Pythagoras. You may find people from all over the world staying on Rhodes. Its beaches and the town of Lindhos, with its fortress rising above the white houses, are impressive. A visit to the Valley of the Butterflies to see the amazing swarms of golden moths that settle in the wooded valley is a must. Large or small, near or far, each island has something unique to offer.

Journey into the Past

Crete is the largest island in Greece and the most southerly one. It is a mountainous place with many farms, seaport towns and small villages. Since there is often not enough water to grow crops, large white windmills with canvas sails are used to pump underground water onto the land.

One of the things that makes Crete so famous are the people who lived there in the past. Nearly 5000 years ago, when many Europeans were living in primitive conditions, the people of Crete had fabulous five-story palaces with toilets that flushed. They were known as Minoans and their civilization, centered at Knossos, flourished for hundreds of years. As well as being great sailors who traded throughout the Mediterranean region, they made beautiful pottery and jewelry. The abrupt end to the Minoan civilization came, it is thought, when a nearby volcano erupted, causing a terrible earthquake.

Ruins of this ancient civilization can still be seen on Crete. There are temples, villas and the remains of palaces. And from the fresco paintings that are still being uncovered much can be learned of daily life back then.

A morning ride through the breathtaking mountain scenery of Crete.

Did you know . . .
Crete has no poisonous snakes.

Welcome, Stranger

In northern Greece, you may need a warm sweater or coat during winter months, but it's never too cold to play outside with a friend.

Xenos means stranger in Greek and it also means guest. If you visit Greece, chances are you will not feel like a *xenos* for long. That's because the Greeks will very quickly make you feel at home. In stores, people will smile at you and kids on the street will wave. If you start talking to them, they might invite you to play soccer or even home for dinner.

Young and old alike will be eager to try their English on you. They will also want to hear your ideas about many things. Finding out how others think is important to Greeks. So don't be surprised by all their questions.

Greece is a beautiful land of sandy beaches, peaceful farms and bustling towns. If you are lucky enough to go see it for yourself some day, the warmth of the people will make you wish you never had to leave. But even if you do not have the chance to go there, you can see the Greek message of friendship when it is sent to the world every four years with the Olympic flame.

Fast Facts

Area:	131 944 km^2 (50,944 sq. mi.)
Population:	9 965 830 (1986 estimate)
Capital:	Athens
Highest Point:	Mount Olympus, 2917 m (9,570 ft.)
Language:	Greek
Currency:	Drachma (= 100 lepta)
National Holidays:	March 25, Independence Day October 28, National Day
Religion:	Eastern Orthodox

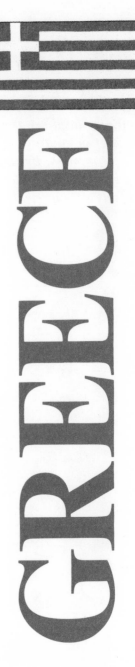

Fun Facts

- The Greek Olympic Games were considered so important that all wars stopped for them.

- Several open air theaters built over 2000 years ago are still used for performances.

- Along the coast of the island of Serifos are rocks that resemble human beings. They are said to be the victims of Medusa, a frightful monster the mere sight of whom turned people to stone.

- *The Jockey*, the ancient bronze statue seen on page 31, was found in the sea near Athens.

- Greeks refer to themselves as Hellenes and to their country as Hellas.

Words to Know

Backgammon
A board game for two in which pieces are moved according to throws of dice.

Bouzouki
A popular Greek instrument with six metal strings.

Fresco
Painting done in water-color on plaster that is still wet so that the colors sink into the plaster.

Kiosk
A small street corner shop that sells a wide variety of small items.

Lent
Period of fasting and prayer that Christian churches observe before Easter.

Mythology
Collection of traditional stories about superhuman beings.

Orthodox
Refers to a branch of the Christian faith practiced in Greece and other countries of eastern Europe and the Middle East.

Philosopher
A person who studies the nature and purpose of life and the universe. The most famous Greek philosophers were Socrates, Plato and Aristotle.

Xenos
Greek word meaning both *stranger* and *guest*.

Index

Photo Credits